Worries Are Not Forever

Elizabeth Verdick

Illustrated by Marieka Heinlen

free spirit
PUBLISHING®

Text copyright © 2019 by Elizabeth Verdick
Illustrations copyright © 2019 by Marieka Heinlen

Library of Congress Cataloging-in-Publication Data
This book has been filed with the Library of Congress: ISBN 978-1-63198-314-6.
LCCN 2018008123.

Free Spirit Publishing does not have control over or assume responsibility for author or third-party websites and their content.

Reading Level Grade 1; Interest Level Ages 4–7;
Fountas & Pinnell Guided Reading Level J

Cover and interior design by Shannon Pourciau

10 9 8 7 6 5 4 3 2 1
Printed in China
R18860618

Free Spirit Publishing Inc.
6325 Sandburg Road, Suite 100
Minneapolis, MN 55427-3674
(612) 338-2068
help4kids@freespirit.com
www.freespirit.com

To anyone—young or young at heart—who
has ever felt worried. I hope this book
provides words of comfort for children,
and ways to help for adults.
—E.V.

To my children, Levi and Nora.
—M.H.

The world is a big, beautiful place.

So much to see and do!

Sometimes BIG
feels a little scary.

3

BIG
rides

BIG animals

BIG
classrooms

BIG
challenges

And sometimes BIG worries . . . even if you're excited at the same time.

What are *worries*?

Worries are thoughts like:
Something bad might happen.
I might make a mistake.
I can't do this.

Worried thoughts make your heart beat faster.

Your stomach feels like it's full of butterflies.

Guess what?

You are bigger than your worries.

You can learn to make your worries smaller and smaller and smaller.

How? Start with knowing that lots of kids feel worried.

You're not alone.

They worry about loud
noises and dark places,
new people to meet and
new things to try.

13

Everybody worries—even grown-ups.
"Do you worry, Dad?"

14

"Sure I do.
It's okay to
feel that way."

15

Worries are not forever.

There are many ways to help your worries go away.

Worries don't last as long if you *talk* about them . . .

to a parent

a brother, sister, or babysitter

18

19

Moving around can make your worries move away.

Run

Climb

Jump

20

You'll start to feel better.

Dance

Stretch!

Keeping your *hands* busy helps, too.

Play with clay   Draw or paint

Build with blocks

Dig in the sand

Wave goodbye to those worries!

23

Whenever you need to
calm yourself down,
take a few *deep breaths*.

Breathe in slowly through your nose,
like you're smelling cookies.

Breathe out slowly through your mouth,
like you're blowing bubbles.

Picture a place
that makes you feel peaceful.

If it helps, you can repeat these words to yourself:

"Worries are not forever.
Worries are not forever."

27

When you're worried,
you might need
a *big hug*.

28

Cuddle someone you love.

Snuggle something soft.

Ahhhhh

Now, think
good thoughts:
I am fine.
I am calm.
I am safe.

Worries are not forever . . .

If they come back, you know just what to do.

Tips and Activities for Caregivers and Parents

All children worry—some more than others. Adults may see children's worries as small or insignificant, but worries and fears are very real for children. If children believe their fears will lead to something bad happening, physical and emotional stress may result. You can read the body language and behaviors that may signal stress. Signs include:

- being tearful or clingy
- restlessness, agitation, pacing, fidgeting, outbursts, aggression
- being tired during the day or having difficulty sleeping at night
- not being able to focus in class
- a change in appetite
- avoidance of school, social occasions, or everyday activities
- biting nails, chewing hair, sucking on shirt sleeves

Children may not realize that some of their symptoms are the result of worried thoughts. Find out if your child:

- feels tired or worn down most of the day
- has a faster heartbeat or racing heart
- often gets "butterflies in the stomach"
- feels shaky or sweaty
- has frequent stomachaches or headaches
- gets a restless feeling or can't seem to sit still
- has racing or repetitive thoughts

Getting a child to recognize these signs is a first step in talking about the feelings. A sense of relief will follow . . . but there's more work to do.

Cutting Worries Down to Size

Worries Are Not Forever aims to give children tools for coping with anxious thoughts and feelings. One of the messages of the book is "*You* are bigger than your worries." Children learn that worries are thoughts that can be talked back to.

Together, you can try an activity where your child gives his or her worries a name, such as Worry Bug, Worry Monster, or Sir Worries. What does this character look like? A creepy-crawly? A fuzzy monster? A man with a silly mustache? Help your child bring the character to life in a drawing or by making a puppet, a painted rock creature, or a clay sculpture. This character can be held in the hands and spoken to: "Stop bugging me," "Goodbye, monster," "Sir, it's time for you to go to bed."

Other ways to "put away worries" include:

Make a worry jar: Decorate a jar and ask your child to write worries on slips of paper to "take out of your head and place into the jar." You can also use a box or any other container you like. It's a powerful moment when, later on, a child can remove one of the slips of paper, read about a specific worry, and then tear it up because the problem is gone.

Use a worry timer: Set aside some "worry time." If your child worries a lot, allow a certain time of the day to be designated for that purpose only. Set the timer for ten minutes or so. This is the time to let all the worries come out freely. When worry time is over, we "put the worries away for the day." Follow up with a physical activity or something enjoyable to take the mind off of worry.

Give a worry doll: These are tiny handmade Guatemalan dolls (about an inch in size) created from wool, wire, and leftover textiles. Dressed in traditional Mayan style, the dolls derive from the legend of a Mayan princess who, as a gift from the sun god, could solve any problem a person might worry about.

Traditionally, a worry doll was placed under a child's pillow, so the child could "sleep on the problem" and have his or her sorrows taken away. You can give your child a worry doll or make one together. The doll is a "listener" and "helper" and can be used as a tool to facilitate conversations between you and your child.

Talking About Worries

If a child's worry alarm goes off, use that signal to play detective:

- What is the worrisome thought? (Write it down.)
- Are there other thoughts lurking around it? (Put them on paper too.)

- Is this thought about something that might happen in the future? How likely is it to really happen? (Talk to the worries. Challenge them. Look for alternative—positive—scenarios.)
- Is the thought about something that already happened? (Talk about the event and the pain it is causing.)
- Seek comfort. (A safe space, or if that's not possible in the moment, the breathing techniques on page 24 can be used instead.)
- Talk back to the worry. (Use whatever words may be helpful in this situation. Worries are not forever. I am calm. I am safe. I can tame my worries.)

The way that you, as the adult, talk about worry makes a big difference in the lives of the children in your care—so avoid negative language. Hearing "stop" and "don't" won't make the worries go away.

Words That DON'T Help

- ⊘ "Stop worrying."
- ⊘ "There's nothing to worry about."
- ⊘ "Don't be such a worry wart."
- ⊘ "I'm so tired of hearing about your worrying."
- ⊘ "Calm down!"

Words That DO Help

✓ "I'm here to listen."

✓ "Worries are just thoughts, just feelings. We can get through this together."

✓ "You are bigger than your worries. How big does this worry feel?"

✓ "You're safe. Let's talk."

✓ "What can I do to help?"

✓ "Talk to your worry. What do you want to tell it?"

✓ "I feel worried too sometimes. I am here for you."

✓ "You have my support."

✓ "Let's work together, like an anti-worry team."

✓ "Step by step, we will calm ourselves down."

✓ "This feeling won't last forever. I'll stay with you while we work through it."

✓ "Let's walk. Moving can help make worries go away."

✓ "You are not alone."

✓ "I think you're brave. You're facing your worry."

✓ "Let's make a battle cry!"

I won't let my worries get me down!

I am bigger than my worries!

I am strong and I can do this!

I've got this!

Helping Children Calm Down

Set up a quiet space. Whether at home or in the classroom, children enjoy having a safe space to chill out in when stressed. This place can be as simple as a beanbag chair with earphones. Lower the lights, provide pillows, keep books handy . . . teach children that they can go to this space to breathe deep, relax, and feel restored.

Keep worry tools handy. Little things like stress balls, putty, squishy toys, and "fidgets" can help children focus and calm down. So can art supplies, such as clay, markers, and paint. In places where it's not possible to have such tools, ask a child who is stressed to press her hands against the wall, pushing hard against the flat surface to push her worries away.

Practice belly breathing. Belly breathing is a special way of controlling the breath to feel calmer. The trick is to teach this skill ahead of time so children can use it in moments of difficulty.

1. Imagine a balloon on your belly. Put a hand on top of your belly.

2. Breathe in slowly through your nose. As you do this, count to three, pausing between each number (1, pause, 2, pause, 3). Feel the imaginary balloon filling with air.

3. Breathe out slowly through your mouth. Count to five, pausing between each number. Imagine that the balloon is getting flat. Picture your negative feelings leaving your body as you breathe out.

4. Repeat the belly breathing several times. Notice your muscles relaxing and your worried thoughts slowing down.

To enhance belly breathing, give children bubble wands to blow through or pinwheels to move with their breath. These items are usually available at dollar stores.

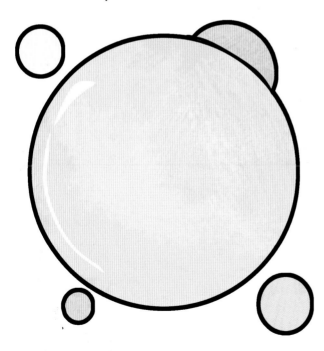

About the Author and Illustrator

Elizabeth Verdick has been writing books since 1997, the year her daughter was born. Her two children are the inspiration for nearly everything she writes. She is the author of more than 40 highly acclaimed books for children and teens in Free Spirit's Best Behavior, Toddler Tools, Happy Healthy Baby, and Laugh and Learn series. Some of her most beloved titles include *Germs Are Not for Sharing*, *Words Are Not for Hurting*, *Calm-Down Time*, *Don't Behave Like You Live in a Cave*, *Stress Can Really Get on Your Nerves*, and *The Survival Guide for Kids with Autism Spectrum Disorders (and Their Parents)*. She lives with her husband, two children, and a houseful of pets near St. Paul, Minnesota.

Marieka Heinlen received her BFA at the University of Wisconsin, Madison, and also studied at Central Saint Martins College of Art and Design in London. She launched her career as an award-winning children's book illustrator with *Hands Are Not for Hitting* and has illustrated all of the books in the Best Behavior and Toddler Tools series. Marieka focuses her work on books and other materials for children, teens, parents, and teachers. She lives in St. Paul, Minnesota, with her husband, son, and daughter.

Best Behavior® English-Spanish Editions

Board Books for Ages 0–3

Paperbacks for Ages 4–7

Board Book

Board Book

Board Book

Paperback — Board Book

Paperback — Board Book

Paperback — Board Book

Paperback — Board Book

Interested in purchasing multiple quantities and receiving volume discounts?
Contact edsales@freespirit.com or call 1.800.735.7323 and ask for Education Sales.

Many Free Spirit authors are available for speaking engagements, workshops, and keynotes.
Contact speakers@freespirit.com or call 1.800.735.7323.

For pricing information, to place an order, or to request a free catalog, contact:
Free Spirit Publishing Inc. • toll-free 800.735.7323 • help4kids@freespirit.com • www.freespirit.com